Introduction

The former Mid Wales county of Radnorshire includes a wide range of nature reserves and conservation areas. To the south of Radnorshire lies the Wye Valley, in or near which can be found a number of reserves – several areas of woodland, wildfowl winter feeding grounds and a 'roadside' reserve made up of varied stretches of verge and adjacent ground. Nearby can be found the Begwns, open access hill grazing owned by the National Trust, which provides excellent views to south and north.

In the mid-section of the county, between Llandrindod Wells and Kington (just into Herefordshire), reserves include a waterfall gorge with nearby Victorian features, upland moor and wetland, further woodland and a common frequented by ground-nesting birds. Continuing to the northern edge of the county leads to Presteigne, the setting for one of the two 'urban' walks combining meadows, riverside and woodlands. Moving to the north and west leads to Beacon Hill Crown Estate (managed by Radnorshire Wildlife Trust), a substantial area of open moorland, crossed by Glyndŵr's Way. The area around Rhayader includes a working organic farm with a wide variety of habitats, further woodland, some within the Elan Valley itself and areas of open hill land. Rhayader is the setting for the second 'urban' walk which includes riverside walks, a churchyard with rare plant and lichen species and an 'edge of town' reserve that includes a bat tunnel.

This is by no means an exhaustive collection of all the nature reserves and conservation areas to be found in and around Radnorshire. The large conservation area in and around the Elan Valley (much of it owned by the Elan Valley Estate, the National Trust and the RSPB) has only been touched on in the Elan Valley Woods walk. There are also a number of Forestry Commission Wales sites, chiefly based along the A44(T), A488, in the Abbey Cwmhir area and near Presteigne that include walking routes (subject to forestry operational requirements). Additional details of the reserves and conservation areas included in this guide, together with information about other local reserves, can be obtained from the websites of the relevant nature trusts and conservation organisations (see the details at the start of each of the walks in this guide).

The use of walking boots and suitable clothing for the routes contained in this guide is recommended. Walkers are advised to check weather forecasts, particularly if following upland paths (09068 505 315). The location of each walk and its starting point is shown on and inside the back cover, together with estimated walking times (the latter have been based on the assumption that walkers will wish to pause to observe and record the wildlife seen on route). Public transport links have been included when currently available – details of these can be checked on 0845 607 6060. Allow extra time if exploring some of the places of interest near the routes. Please follow the country code (as some of the reserves may be used for grazing at certain times, always keep dogs on leads) – and enjoy your walking!

CARN GAFALLT & DOLIFOR WOOD

DESCRIPTION There is considerable variety on this moderate 3¾ mile walk (with optional extension of up to 1½ miles), that starts by following the Wye Valley Walk from the village of Llanwrthl. A fairly steep initial climb leads to a range of excellent views from RSPB open hill land (Carn Gafallt reserve). There is an opportunity to follow a well-used bridleway along a section of the hill reserve, before returning to the Wye Valley Walk and starting down towards the next valley. After a short while, the route leaves the long distance trail to enter Woodland Trust property at Dolifor, which is maily comprised of oak and birch, with blocks of conifers in the upper southern side of the wood. Paths through this mixed woodland pass through a range of habitats, allowing views towards Rhayader on route and providing a number of benches from which to enjoy these. Beyond Dolifor Wood, a footpath leads down to the River Elan and follows this to the junction with the Wye, meeting the Wye Valley Walk on route. The return journey to Llanwrthl makes use of a quiet lane passing fields and woods, alongside which drystone walling (a habitat now rare in some parts of Britain) can frequently be seen. Allow up to 3 hours for the main walk, up to 1¼ hours for the extension.

WEBSITES www.rspb.org.uk, www.woodland-trust.org.uk

START Llanwrthl Village, just off the A470(T), south of Rhayader, SN 976637.

I Follow the road into the village and round to the right when near the church (signed Elan Village 4½ miles on the right). Continue along the road and take the right fork at the next junction. Follow the road for a few more yards and then turn RIGHT on an off-road section of the Wye Valley Walk. Follow the path up to a lane and turn LEFT. In a few yards, turn RIGHT, following Wye Valley Walk waymarking. Go through a gate on the right and follow the track uphill,

round to the left and past farm buildings, via two gates. Continue ahead for about ¼ mile to a Wye Valley Walk/bridleway waymark post. *At this point there is the option of following the bridleway along the hill for further excellent views and moorland bird life, before returning to the waymark post.*

2 Turn RIGHT (or LEFT if returning from the optional extension along the hill). Go past the entrance to Pen-y-rhiw (on the left). On reaching woodland, also on the left, look out for a Woodland Trust sign. Turn LEFT here and cross the stile into Dolifor Wood. Follow the path ahead, crossing a rustic footbridge. At two waymark posts on right, continue AHEAD. Go past two benches on the left. On nearing a gate out of the wood, turn SHARP RIGHT and follow the path alongside the fence. When the fence turns left, by a

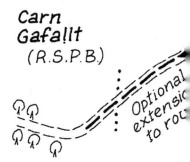

Carn Gafallt (R.S.P.B.)

Optional extension to route

waymark post, also turn LEFT. Pass a field gate on the left and cross an old bank. Cross a low-growing tree trunk.

3 Continue to follow the path and bear LEFT at a waymark post on the right. At the fence turn RIGHT and follow path to right of fence. By a gate on the left, go RIGHT on path. At a fork in the path, by a bench on the right, go LEFT. Follow the path down to the left. At the waymark post on the right and the gate on the left, turn SHARP RIGHT. Go past a Woodland Trust information board on the left. Continue AHEAD on the path, past a bench on the right. Head LEFT at a fork in the track, leading down to a stile out of the wood.

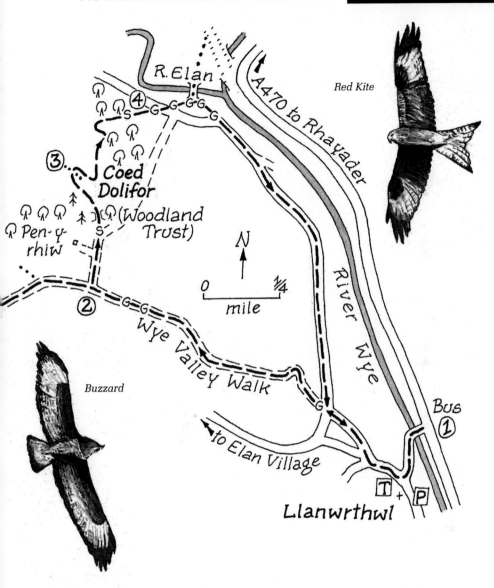

R. Elan

A470 to Rhayader

Red Kite

③

④

Coed Dolifor

Pen-y-rhiw

(Woodland Trust)

N

0   ¼
    mile

River Wye

②

Wye Valley Walk

Buzzard

to Elan Village

Bus
①

T + P

Llanwrthwl

4 Go HALF LEFT along the field to a gate onto a lane. Turn RIGHT. After a few yards, go through a gate on the left. Follow the path down to the left of buildings. Pass through two gates to the right of a footbridge. Continue AHEAD on the riverside path to the junction of the Elan and Wye. Follow the path and then track to the right to reach a gate and then a lane. Turn LEFT and follow the lane for just over a mile, passing Dyffryn Farm B&B on the left. At the Wye Valley Walk waymark post, go LEFT down the path. At the road, turn LEFT and retrace the route back past Llanwrthl Church.

TOWN PARKS, RIVERSIDE WALK, CHURCHYARD & RHAYADER BAT TUNNEL RESERVE

DESCRIPTION This easy walk of 3 miles around Rhayader takes in a riverside path where Common Sandpipers, Goosander, Grey Wagtails and Kingfishers can be seen, together with a variety of fish and invertebrate species. From here, the route continues through a pleasant riverside park and visits a church in the eaves of which Long Eared and Pipistrelle bats roost. The churchyard has other features of interest, including 100 species of flowering plants and 110 species of lichen. This is one of the 19 Radnorshire sites in which bistort is found. The walk continues out of Rhayader and onto the Elan Valley Trail to visit Radnorshire Wildlife Trust's Rhayader Tunnel Reserve. The area around the former railway tunnel, used by bats in winter, is also an autumn feeding ground for finches and other birds, such as Redstarts and Tawny Owls. The final part of the walk leads back into town and goes via another park, where is the option to follow a further riverside path before returning to Dark Lane past the site of Rhayader Castle. Allow up to 2½ hours for the walk. *When walking the churchyard section, please follow the requests with regard to visitors during times when services are in progress.*
WEBSITES www.radnorshirewildlifetrust.org. uk, www.churchinwales.org.uk
START Dark Lane car park, SN 971683

I Go RIGHT out of Dark Lane car park. Almost immediately, turn LEFT. Go past the Leisure Centre, on the left. Continue along the street (North Street) towards the centre of town. Go past the town clock and continue AHEAD on South Street (signposted for Builth Wells/Newbridge-on-Wye). Go past the '40' speed limit sign. Look out for

the Riverside Walk waymark post on the right. Follow this down past white railings and a house to the river bank.

2 Turn RIGHT and follow the riverside route (this includes a shingle bank alongside the Wye). Towards the end of the route, continue along a track and bear LEFT on the access track to playing fields on the right. At the tarmac lane, go LEFT. Follow the lane round to the right and up to West Street. Turn LEFT and follow the road over the Wye Bridge and round to the left. Take the first turning on the left and go down the steps to the left of the toilets. Turn HALF RIGHT and follow the path alongside the Wye. At the end of the park, double back and head for gates into the lane below the church.

3 Bear RIGHT up the lane, taking the left fork to go past the 16th century Triangle Inn. Follow the lane round to the left to reach the churchyard gates on the left. Follow path around churchyard and exit via main gates when ready. Turn LEFT and LEFT again at the main road. Follow the main road to the ornate gates at the start of the Elan Valley Trail. Go LEFT through the gates and follow the path up to and through a further two gates. Almost immediately, go through a third gate on the left. After a few feet, follow a path HALF LEFT up the bank and round to the right. Follow a narrow path through trees and then continue along a broad grassy area. At the end, bear RIGHT and go through a gate on the left. Head RIGHT to the Elan Valley Trail and Radnorshire Wildlife Trust noticeboard.

4 Go LEFT on the Elan Valley Trail, which bends left and then right, before beginning to descend. Look out for and go down steps on the right. The area of the bat tunnel can be seen to the right. When ready, head along the old railway line away from the bat tunnel. Go through a gate back onto the Elan Valley Trail. Turn LEFT and follow the trail back to the road. Follow the road to the right and back over the Wye Bridge. Take the first turn on the left and follow the lane round to the left. Cross a small car park and follow the riverside path between fencing and out-

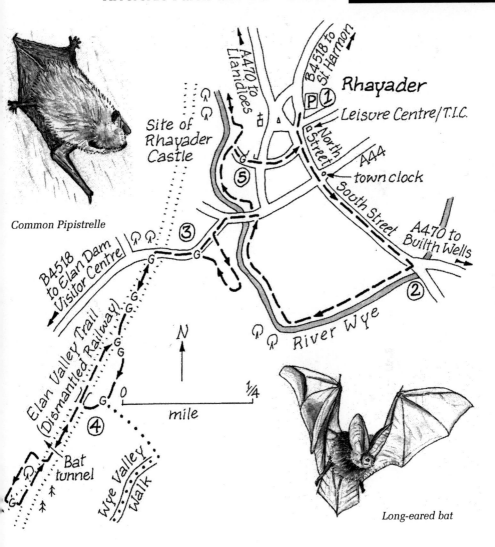

Common Pipistrelle

Long-eared bat

cropping to Waun Capel Park. On reaching the play area, follow one of the two options below:

A Cross the footbridge on the left and turn RIGHT. Follow the riverside path as far as the fence and then return to and recross the footbridge. Head HALF RIGHT up the hill, signposted for the Castle Site and Town Centre.

B Turn SHARP RIGHT and follow the path up the hill, signposted for the Castle Site and Town Centre.

5 Go through the gates onto Castle Street (the castle site is to the right, beyond gates). Continue AHEAD on Castle Street, crossing the junction into Cross Lane. Continue AHEAD to North Street. Go over pedestrian crossing, turn LEFT and then RIGHT to return to Dark Lane car park.

ELAN VALLEY WOODLAND

DESCRIPTION Following a short walk alongside a picturesque section of the Elan, this moderate 3 mile route crosses the river and follows a zig-zag nature trail, with frequent interpretation boards, climbing steadily past a variety of trees, then past patches of heather and gorse. The upper reaches of the route provide excellent views over the Elan valley. From the top of the nature trail, the walk follows a permissive path down through broadleaved woods to the area around the Elan Village, where it follows a roughly triangular route comprised of two quiet roads and a footpath, following the Elan river for a short way and passing through RSPB woods. A wide variety of birds can be seen in and around the Elan Valley and this is an excellent site for woodland flowers in spring as well as lower plants to be seen in the oak woods. The route then returns to the entrance to the nature trail and retraces the route to the Elan Valley Visitor Centre. Allow up to 2½ hours for the walk.
WEBSITES www.elanvalley.org.uk, www.rspb.org.uk
START Elan Valley Visitor Centre, south west of Rhayader, SN 928646.

I Head along the grassy area to the right of the first part of the driveway up from the Visitor Centre. Go RIGHT over the road bridge towards the Elan Village. Once over the bridge, bear HALF RIGHT and continue AHEAD between wooden railings to a gate into Cnwch Wood.

2 Follow the path round to the right by the first interpretation board. Bear LEFT near the 'Willow' interpretation board. After a short distance, turn RIGHT. Go LEFT just after the 'Birch' interpretation board and RIGHT just after the 'Rowan' board. At the next (unmarked) turn, bear LEFT.

3 At the end of the trail, cross the stile and go LEFT between fences. Go through a gate and follow the permissive path down through the woods. Cross over a footpath (near a gate and footbridge on the right) and continue AHEAD through a gate and past the Elan Lodge to reach the Elan Village road. Turn RIGHT and follow the road over a cattle grid and to a T-junction.

4 Turn RIGHT along a road now bordered by RSPB woods. Continue until reaching a footpath sign on the right. Turn RIGHT and follow the footpath down to the second waymark sign and turn LEFT. Follow the path down, over a footbridge and through a gate.

5 Cross over the permissive path followed earlier and continue AHEAD, with a fence to the right. Cross a stile and turn RIGHT through a gate out of Cnwch Wood. Cross back over the road bridge and turn LEFT to return to the Visitor Centre.

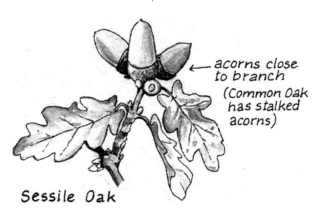

← acorns close
to branch
(Common Oak
has stalked
acorns)

Sessile Oak

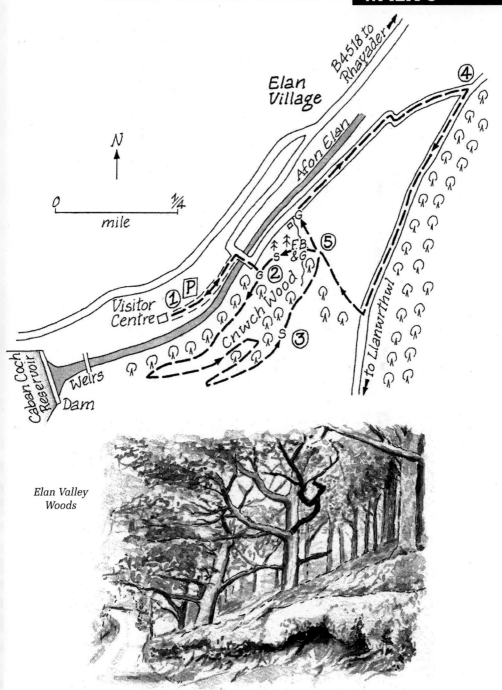

B4518 to Rhayader

Elan Village

Afon Elan

N

0 — ¼ mile

Elan Village

④

⑤

FB & G

G

S

G ②

Crwch Wood

③

S

to Llanwrthwl

Visitor Centre ①

P

Caban Coch Reservoir

Weirs

Dam

Elan Valley Woods

GILFACH FARM RESERVE

DESCRIPTION Gilfach Farm Visitor Centre, owned by Radnorshire Wildlife Trust, is set in the beautiful surroundings of the Marteg valley. An organic farm, grazed by sheep and beef cattle, Gilfach escaped the modernisation of farming during the last century. The Visitor Centre, which provides hot and cold drinks, organic icecream and crisps, plus homemade bara brith, includes a Wildlife Trust shop. Adjacent to the centre, a converted barn, is a restored longhouse of the traditional type. There is a choice of routes comprised of some 5½ miles in total, taking in riverside, hill and woodland settings. The suggested route below (of about 3½ miles) combines part of the Nature Trail with the Monk's Trod Trail, then passes the Visitor Centre on route for the Oakwood Path. It is a mainly easy route with one ascent. A variety of bird life, mammals, invertebrates, trees and other plants can be found in the valley, as well as some great views. A free leaflet, available from Gilfach Visitor Centre, provides additional details of the walks and Gilfach Farm buildings. Allow up to 3 hours for the walk.
WEBSITE www.radnorshirewildlifetrust.org.uk
START Gilfach Farm Visitor Centre, north of Rhayader and between A470(T) and B4518, SN 965718.

▮ The Nature Trail

This route follows the Wye Valley Walk (and the course of an old railway line). The key features of this route include the variety of habitats created by the former railway line. Frequent information boards give details of the history, geology and natural features of the route. From the Visitor Centre car park, go LEFT down the drive to join the Nature Trail just beyond the bridge over the Marteg. Turn LEFT and go through a gate with yellow waymarking (the standard colour for this route). Follow the riverside path across five fields, connected by gates. Cross two waymarked stiles to join the course of the

old railway line (with a bat tunnel off to the right). Follow the course of the old railway line, eventually going up steps on the right Turn LEFT and follow the rest of the Nature Trail to the junction with a main road. (The route of the Nature Trail bears RIGHT along the verge and over the Marteg Bridge, then turns RIGHT again to return to the drive up to the Visitor Centre. To avoid road walking, follow stage **2** below).

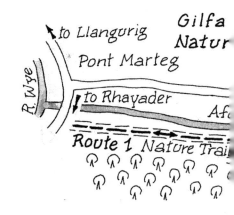

2 The Monk's Trod Trail

This route follows part of the course of an old route between Abbey Cwmhir and Strata Florida Abbey. The scenery is a mixture of organic meadows and hill grazing. To join the Monk's Trod Trail, start by retracing part of the route along the Nature Trail. Descend the steps and turn LEFT. Once past the diversion around a damp area of old railway bed, look out for a waymark post on the right. Bear RIGHT here onto the path through the trees. Cross a stile and turn RIGHT. Follow the path uphill and then turn LEFT by a waymark post (red is the standard colour for the Monk's Trod Trail) near a gate on the right. Follow the path along the hill, passing benches, and then across fields and a wooded track, connected by gates. Go through a final gate and turn RIGHT to go up the top part of the drive to the Visitor Centre.

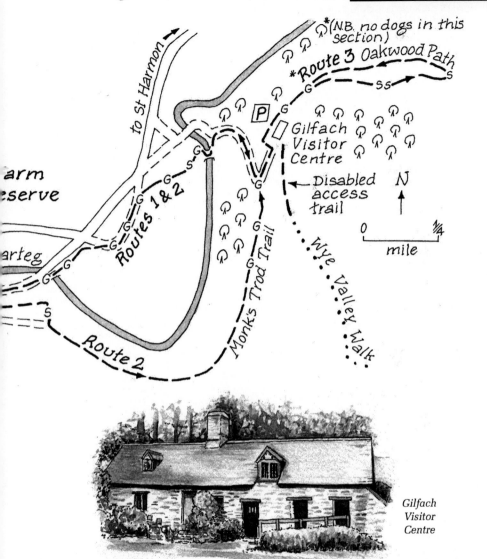

*Gilfach
Visitor
Centre*

3 The Oakwood Path

This route starts from just outside the Visitor Centre and leads across fields to enter a large oak wood – a good site for bluebells in the spring. The path leads along the wood and then returns via fields that provide excellent views across the valley. From outside the shop, turn RIGHT and go through a gate with green waymarking. Follow the path down to the right and go through another gate. Bear RIGHT along the field to a stile. Head up to a track and turn LEFT. Cross a stile to the right of a gate and follow the waymarked path through the oak wood, eventually exiting via a stile on the left. Turn LEFT and follow the waymarked route across four fields, connected by gates to rejoin the outward route. Folllow the track for a short way, then descend to the RIGHT to retrace the route along the left hand side of the field to return to the Visitor Centre.

CEFN CENARTH NORTH & SOUTH

DESCRIPTION This moderate walk of some 2 miles, plus optional lane extension of 2 miles, follows a path around a traditional oak woodland, on a hillside setting. The view from the walking route has recently been improved by forestry clearance, which alllows sight of the hills that skirt this attractive valley. The reserve is in two parts – Cefn Cenarth South and North, with paths only present in the latter. The reserves are mainly oak woodland, with some rowan and larch. Plants that can be seen include bilberry, bracken, common bent-grass, heath bedstraw and wavy hair-grass, with an underlayer of mosses. Cefn Cenarth South tends to have a wider range of other higher plants, although common cow-wheat, slender St John's wort and wood sorrel can be found in Cefn Cenarth North. Thirty two bird species nest on the reserves, where nest boxes have been provided – pied flycatcher and redstart make use of these. Other birds that may be seen include blackcap, chiffchaff, coal tits, garden warbler, long-tailed tits, marsh tits, willow tits, willow warbler and wood warbler. Invertebratre species consist of those often found in Welsh oak woodland. *The path around Cefn Cenarth North includes steep ascents and descents for which suitable footware is essential. Please keep dogs on a lead when visiting reserves.* Radnorshire Wildlife Trust has recently bought more woodland and is improving the reserve,

WEBSITE www.radnorshirewildlifetrust.org.uk

START Either roadside parking at Pant-y-dwr, SN 983751 OR roadside parking at old quarry site, SN 965756.

1 From the B4518 at Pant-y-dwr, take the lane leading west for about 1¼ miles, passing the disused quarry site towards the end of the route. Walkers on this section of the route will pass Cefn Cenarth South Nature Reserve, on the right. Although

there are no paths, it is possible to view this reserve from the lane, together with attractive open hill views on the other side of the valley. Once at the quarry, continue west on the lane for a short way.

2 When the lane bends to the left, look out for the track on the right leading to Tan-yr-allt. Follow the track past the house and into the forestry area. Follow the main track for about ¼ mile, until reaching an unmarked junction of main tracks. Take the right hand fork, which soon leads past a Radnorshire Wildlife Trust waymark sign on the left. Continue along the track looking out for a further waymark sign on the right.

3 Go through the gate on the right and up to the information board. From this point, follow the waymark posts (with white arrows) on a zig-zag path that climbs steeply through the reserve and then follows a short and more level route to the right. *The path on the first part of the descent is initially not very clear to follow – the best route is to zig-zag downhill, using the boundary fence on the left as a visual reference point.* On reaching a clearer section of the path, follow this down hill and then bear right on a level track that leads back to the information board and exit. Follow the forestry track and then lane route back to Pant-y-dwr.

Thin call. High pitched. 'teechu-teechu-teechu.'

Coal Tit
(11-12cm)
Black head, white cheek, bright buff underside.

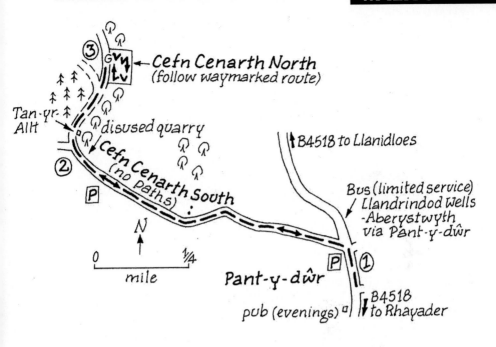

3 G ← **Cefn Cenarth North**
(follow waymarked route)

Tan-yr-Allt

disused quarry

Cefn Cenarth South
(no paths)

2

P

↑ B4518 to Llanidloes

Bus (limited service)
Llandrindod Wells
-Aberystwyth
via Pant-y-dŵr

N

0 ——— ¼
mile

Pant-y-dŵr

P 1

B4518
to Rhayader

pub (evenings)

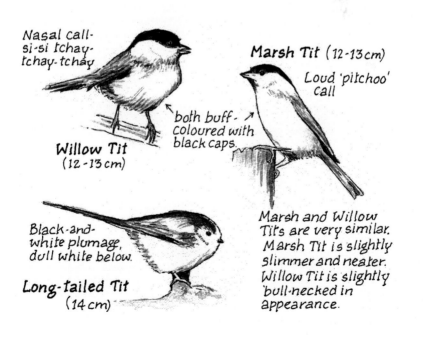

Nasal call-
si-si tchay-
tchay-tchay

Marsh Tit (12-13 cm)

Loud 'pitchoo'
call

← both buff-
coloured with
black caps.

Willow Tit
(12-13 cm)

Black-and-
white plumage,
dull white below.

Long-tailed Tit
(14 cm)

Marsh and Willow
Tits are very similar.
Marsh Tit is slightly
slimmer and neater.
Willow Tit is slightly
'bull-necked in
appearance.

11

WALK 6
HUNDRED HOUSE COMMON & WERNDRYD

DESCRIPTION An easy and leisurely 3 or 3¾ mile walk across a small area of open access common land, followed by a quiet lane edged for most of the way by verges with spring flowers, hedges and trees. Radnorshire Wildlife Trust's Werndryd Nature Reserve itself is a mixture of hedges, wet pasture, ponds and ditches, crossed by a well-used path that includes a boardwalk section. Features of interest include hedges with nesting birds, a range of butterfly species, palmate and smooth newts, dragonflies and damselflies. The longer version of the walk follows further attractive and quiet lanes and crosses a bridge over the River Edw. The shorter version retraces the route to Hundred House. Allow up to 2½ hours for the walk.
WEBSITE www.radnorshirewildlifetrust.org.uk
START Hundred House Common (alongside A481), SO 113544.

Smooth Newt or Common Newt

♂

Length to 11 cm.
Widespread and common, often found in garden ponds.
Breeding males are very showy, with a wavy crest along their back and tail (not spiky as larger Great Crested Newt).
Bright orange-yellow, spotted underparts.

Palmate Newt

♂

Length to 9 cm
Very similar to Smooth Newt.
Breeding males develop black webs on their back feet (from which the newt gets its name).
Pale yellow underparts and unspotted throat.
Favours shallow, acidic water.

1 From the car park, head along Hundred House Common, walking roughly parallel to the lane. At the end of the Common, continue AHEAD along the lane. Pass 'Rhiw View' on the right and a bench on the left (there are good hill views from here).

2 Go past a junction with a lane coming from the left. At the next junction, go RIGHT following a signpost to 'Franksbridge, ¼ mile'. Continue into the village, crossing the road bridge and following the lane uphill past the chapel and the Manse.

3 Go past another junction with a lane coming from the left. Immediately afterwards go through the gate on the left (Radnorshire Wildlife Trust's noticeboard is just inside the reserve). Follow the linear path, including boardwalk section, across the reserve and exit by the far gate.

4

3 mile option
Turn LEFT and follow the lane past the school. Turn LEFT at the junction and RIGHT at the next junction. Retrace the outward route through Franksbridge. At the junction with the 'Franksbridge ¼ sign' go LEFT. Follow the lane back to Hundred House Common.

3¾ mile option
Turn LEFT and follow the lane past the school. Turn RIGHT at the junction and follow the lane past Bettws Mill, on the right, and cross the Edw Bridge. At the junction, turn LEFT. Continue along the lane, ignoring side turnings, to go past the junction with the 'Franksbridge ¼ mile' sign. Continue AHEAD to Hundred House Common.

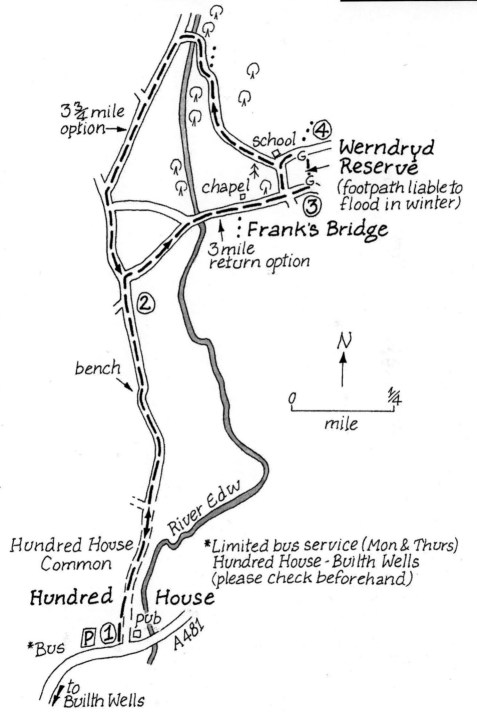

3¾ mile option→

school ④

Werndryd Reserve
(footpath liable to flood in winter)

chapel

③

↑ : Frank's Bridge
3 mile return option

②

bench

N

0 ¼
mile

River Edw

Hundred House Common

*Limited bus service (Mon & Thurs)
Hundred House - Builth Wells
(please check beforehand)

Hundred House

pub

P ① A481

*Bus

to Builth Wells

SIDELAND & PENYBONT COMMON

DESCRIPTION This easy walk of about 3 miles (plus open access common land) follows a road and then a permissive path to Sideland, one of Radnorshire Wildlife Trust's woodland reserves. Here a waymarked path leads alongside the boundaries of the wood, passing through bluebell-rich glades where Early Purple Orchid and a variety of other plants can also be seen. Species of woodland birds such as Bullfinch, Great Spotted Woodpecker, Green Woodpecker, Marsh Tit, Pied Flycatcher, Redstart, Treecreeper and Willow Warbler can be sighted here. There are also wood mice and bank voles, together with large numbers of beetles and butteflies. After visiting the wood, the route leads back to the village, where Penybont Common provides an interesting contrast – being a habitat for ground nesting birds. NB There can be damp areas, particularly towards the east of the Common. Allow up to 3 hours for the walk.
WEBSITE www.radnorshirewildlifetrust.org.uk
START Roadside parking at Penybont on the A44, SO 116642

1 From Penybont, follow the A44 in the direction of Crossgates. Cross the Ithon Bridge. Continue past the first turning on the left and the Hall (behind trees to the left). Turn LEFT on the second minor road, which is signposted for 'Beljays Kennels and Cattery'. Go past two houses on the left. Look out for and turn LEFT into the access drive to Beljays/Cwmrhocas Farm. Follow the drive for a short way, until reaching two adjacent gates on the right.

2 Go through the right hand gate (not waymarked but a permissive path, described in the Trust's leaflet on the reserve). Follow the left hand boundary of the field to reach a second gate. Go through and continue AHEAD to the site of the old field boundary, of which only the trees remain. Go through

the gap in the trees, to the left of a large oak. After a short distance, turn LEFT through a gate. Turn RIGHT and continue AHEAD to reach the gate into the reserve. Follow the circular waymarked path around the reserve, the course of which is indicated by yellow topped waymarked posts.

3 On leaving the reserve, follow the left boundary of the field. Go through the gate on the left and turn RIGHT. Retrace the route across the fields to Beljays drive. Turn LEFT and go RIGHT on the minor road, back to the main road. Cross the road with care and head RIGHT on the pavement. Cross the Ithon Bridge. Turn LEFT and cross the waymarked stile. Go down the steps and head for a gate in the far right hand corner of the field.

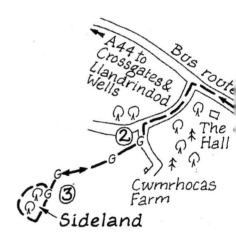

4 Go through the gate and continue to a stile in the far right hand corner of the next field. Cross and bear RIGHT up the bank to a second stile on the left. Cross and head HALF RIGHT up towards the top of the field. When the route of the footpath leads past a gate, turn RIGHT and go through this onto Penybont Common. This is open access land, but a good route for observing ground nesting birds is to bear LEFT past the house and continue uphill and then to the right, making for a circle of trees. Continue along to the edge of the Common and then double back. At

14

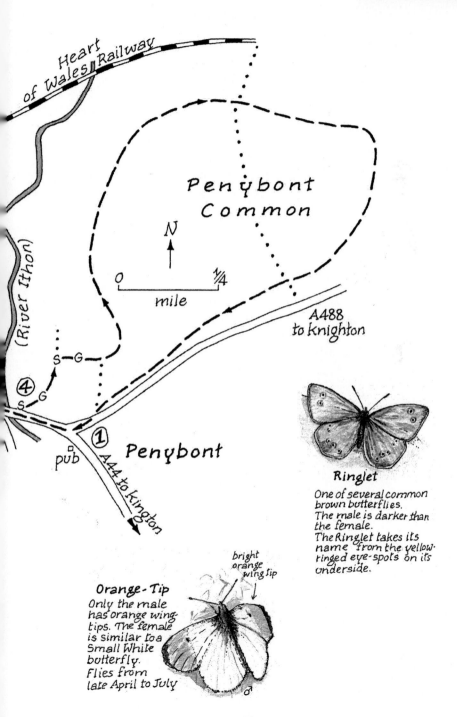

Heart of Wales Railway

Penybont Common

N

0 ¼ mile

A488 to knighton

(River Ithon)

S—G

④ G
S

pub ① Penybont

A44 to kington

Ringlet

One of several common brown butterflies.
The male is darker than the female.
The Ringlet takes its name from the yellow-ringed eye-spots on its underside.

bright orange wing tip

Orange-Tip

Only the male has orange wing-tips. The female is similar to a Small White butterfly.
Flies from late April to July

♂

LLANDEILO GRABAN
ROADSIDE RESERVE

DESCRIPTION An easy 4 mile walk along a beautiful section of the Wye Valley. The route mainly follows a minor road, the verges of which are a nature reserve managed by Radnorshire Wildlife Trust on behalf of Powys County Council. The road follows the course of an old railway line alongside which spring flowers, hedges and trees can be viewed, together with abundant and varied bird and insect life, while there are frequent views across the picturesque Wye Valley. Rock Stonecrop (rare in Radnorshire) can be found here and more than 70 species of lichen have been identified in the wetter areas.

The route also includes an off-road section of the Wye Valley Walk, which passes through a wooded belt close to and allowing excellent views of the River Wye. Erwood Craft Centre, close to the walk, provides light refreshments and has a wide range of attractive locally made crafts on sale. There is also a short riverside walk, starting from near the Craft Centre. Allow up to 3½ hours for the walk.

WEBSITE www.radnorshirewildlifetrust.org.uk.

START Car park near Erwood Craft Centre, about ¼ mile north, off the A470, SO 089438.

3 Cross the stile and bear RIGHT on a clear path that leads under the bridge and over a footbridge. Continue AHEAD through a waymarked gate. Bear LEFT and follow the track through the riverside woods. Continue AHEAD through a further two waymarked gates and eventually bear LEFT to cross a stile back onto the road.

4 Turn left and follow the road back across the 'Weak Bridge'. Continue AHEAD along the road until reaching the car park near the Craft Centre.

1 From the car park, follow the Wye Valley Walk signs to the south-east, across the grass and through a gap in the old fence line. Continue AHEAD over the cattle grid, to the right of John Jones Plant Hire.

2 Follow the road, the verges of which are now part of the reserve, until shortly before reaching a 'Weak Bridge' sign. Look for a Wye Valley Walk waymark post on the left. Bear LEFT at this point and descend a short flight of steps.

WALK 9
WATER-BREAK-ITS-NECK

DESCRIPTION This moderate route of 2½ miles passes through attractive farmland with a spectacular backdrop of hills. The 70 foot waterfall at Water-Break-It's-Neck is impressive in the winter and early spring, while the path along the gorge is a rich location for mosses, ferns and lichens all year round. There are also waymarked paths through the mixed woods around the waterfall area, which includes open sections of heather and other upland plants, with a further sight of the waterfall gorge. This was a popular area for walking in Victorian times and the route crosses one footbridge from that era and comes in sight of another. Woodland birds such as siskin and goldcrest can be seen and there is abundant insect life, including butterflies, in the more open areas. Allow up to 2 hours.

WEBSITE www.forestry.gov.uk/wales

START Parking area west of New Radnor and just off A44, SO 186599.

1 From the A44, follow the access track for about ¾ mile to a parking area on the right (if this is full, there is also parking by the information boards near the main road). Continue along the track on foot. On nearing the footbridge on the right, turn LEFT and follow the path along the waterfall gorge. Then retrace the route back to the track.

2 Cross the main track and go over the footbridge. Follow the broad path round to the right. At the junction of paths, go LEFT, following the direction indicated by a green-banded waymark post. Continue AHEAD at the next waymarked junction.

3 At the next waymark post, on the left, head HALF LEFT on a narrower path. Cross the new footbridge (to the right of the old one) and follow the waymarked path up to the right. Waymarking is currently missing from the next section, but – at a fork in the path – go SHARP LEFT up to a broader track. Turn LEFT and follow this for a short way. Bear HALF RIGHT on a path by a currently fallen waymark post on the right.

4 Follow the path through a more open section that includes blackberry bushes. Descend to and cross over a broad track. Continue downhill. Go past a signed bridleway (currently closed for safety reasons). On reaching a fork in the waymarked route, take the right fork.

5 Follow the steep path uphill and round to the right. On nearing a house on the right, follow the waymarked path HALF LEFT. Descend to and cross a Victorian footbridge. Follow the path back up and continue AHEAD to the right of a fence.

Continue AHEAD down the path through the woods. On reaching the main access track from the A481, follow this back to the start.

17

PWLL PATTI & WYE VALLEY WALK

DESCRIPTION This easy 4¾ mile walk starts by following a scenic road adjacent to a parkland setting and then visits a Radnorshire Wildlife Trust bird watching hide. The hide overlooks water meadows (the former route of the River Wye) used by a wide variety of wildfowl in winter, including Bewick Swan, Coot, Gadwall, Green Sandpiper, Mallard, Mute Swan, Pochard, Teal, Tufted Duck, Water Pipit, Whooper Swan and Widgeon. The reserve is also home to hedge and farmland dwelling bird species, such as Tree Sparrows. From here the route follows a quiet road to join a level section of the Wye Valley Walk on route back to Glasbury. Allow up to 3¼ hours for the walk. *The reserve is best visited in the winter – the fields are grazed in the summer when the meadows dry out.*
WEBSITE www.radnorshirewildlifetrust.org.uk
START Car park alongside B4350, west of Glasbury Bridge, SO 178393

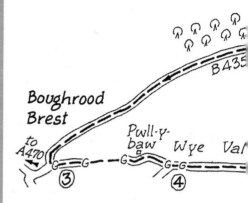

1 From the car parking area, head LEFT on the B4350, signposted for Boughrood and Glasbury. Pass Maesllwch Arms Hotel and a waymark post for the Wye Valley Walk. *The road provides attractive views, particularly of the parkland off to the right.* At Cwmbach, follow the road round to the left, signposted for Boughrood. Continue past two small lay-bys on the left. Enter Pwll Patti hide via the gate on the left. PLEASE USE THE HIDE AS PER THE TRUST'S ON-SITE REQUESTS.

2 Return to the road and head LEFT in the direction of Boughrood for about 1¼ miles, passing pleasant views of fields and woods. Follow the road round a bend to the left by Pistyll (on the right). In a few yards, when the road bends sharply to the right, turn LEFT and go through a gate near a Wye Valley Walk waymark post.

3 Follow the enclosed track and then continue along the left hand side of the field to a gate. Follow the old hedgeline on the left to another gate. Go HALF LEFT past the ruined cottage at Pwll-Baw and follow the track along the left hand side of the field.

4 Go through a gate and bear LEFT on an enclosed track. At the next gate, take the waymarked right fork in the track. Continue along the left hand side of the field, cross a stile and continue to the left of the next long field. On reaching Glasbury Farm, pass to the right of the farm, via three gates.

5 Follow the access track, which draws near to the Wye. Pass through a gate onto a concrete surfaced track. Shortly afterwards head HALF RIGHT off the track (near the waymark post on the left). Head across the field, aiming slightly to the right of a hedge on the far side. Pass to the right of the hedge and fenceline to reach a gate. Go through and follow the track for a short way to the road. Turn RIGHT and follow the road back to Glasbury.

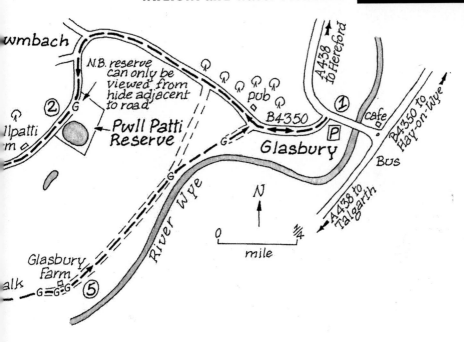

wmbach

N.B. reserve can only be viewed from hide adjacent to road

② G

Ilpatti m

Pwll Patti Reserve

pub

B4350

① cafe

P

Glasbury

Bus

A438 to Hereford

B4350 to Hay-on-Wye

A438 to Talgarth

N

0 ————— ¼ mile

River Wye

Glasbury Farm

alk G=G=G ⑤

Most familiar of the swans. Holds neck in graceful curve. Orange-red bill with distinctive black knob.

Mute Swan

Bewick's Swan

Smaller than Mute & Whooper Swan. Less yellow on bill than Whooper Swan.

Goose-like shaped swans

Whooper Swan

CILCENNI DINGLE & WYE VALLEY WALK

DESCRIPTION Starting from an attractive riverside setting at Glasbury, this moderate 5½ mile route follows the road past scenic parkland to Cwmbach, where it joins a path running through Fishpond Wood and then across Ffynnon Gynydd Common, with its views of the area north of the Wye, to reach Ffynnon Gynydd village. From here a quiet lane leads to a footpath across a field into the Woodland Trust property at Cilcenni Dingle. The footpath crosses the wood and follows its further edge, before crossing fields to reach a lane alongside the top of Brynyrhydd Common. The lane and then a further footpath are used to descend the Common to join the Wye Valley Walk near Brynyrhydd Farm. On the descent towards the A438, there is another opportunity to visit Cilcenni Dingle – using 'there-and-back-again' paths that can be accessed via a gate adjacent to Woodland Trust information board. The Wye Valley Walk, which follows the main road for a short way, before taking to the fields, is used to return to Glasbury. Allow up to 4 hours for the walk.

WEBSITE www.woodland-trust.org.uk

START Glasbury Bridge car park, just off the A438, SO 178393.

1 From the car park, go left along the road towards Cwmbach (*passing parkland views on the right, plus an attractive village setting*). Follow the road until just past Cwmbach Church, on the right, and take the first turn on the right. Almost immediately, cross a footbridge on the right and go through a gate into the wood.

2 Follow the path up through the wood, passing through a second gate. Continue along the path, eventually passing to the left of a house. Cross the drive and continue AHEAD on the waymarked path. Head up the right hand side of Ffynnon Gynydd

Common, passing a waymark post on the brow of the hill. Continue to follow the right hand boundary of the Common, turning LEFT on reaching a gate marked 'Private' on the right. Follow a grassy track along the edge of the Common and then continue AHEAD between hedges. Go past a cottage on the left and cross a stile to the road.

3 Turn SHARP RIGHT and follow a lane out of the village. Continue past the entrance to Maesyronnen Cottages, on the left. At the end of a long field on the left, go through a waymarked gate on the left. Head along the right hand side of the field to a stile into Cilcenni Dingle. Follow the path down to the right and then to the left. Cross steps over a fallen tree and go over a footbridge on the right. Follow the steps up the bank and take the right fork in the path. Cross the area around a ruined dwelling by means of two stiles. Continue on a path through the wood until coming to a stile on the left, into a field.

4 Cross the stile and turn RIGHT. Head along the field to another stile. Cross and follow the left hand boundary of the field to a gate. Pass through and head HALF RIGHT up the next field to a stile in the hedge, some way to the right of a gate. Cross the last field to a stile to the left of a house. Head LEFT along the track, to a gate onto a lane. Go RIGHT along the lane. When the lane bends sharply to the left, follow the waymarked footpath AHEAD. Head down through the wood. On reaching two waymark posts, bear RIGHT. Go through a gate and head LEFT down the lane, past Brynyrhydd Farm.

5 Near the bottom of the hill, look out for a gate on the right, with a Woodland Trust information board nearby. This other entrance into Cilcenni Dingle leads to 'there-and-back-again' paths that can be used to further explore the area if wished (the dingle is too steep for a circular walk to have been created). When ready, continue to and cross the A438 with care and follow the Wye Valley Walk to the right, along the verge. On reaching a gate by Wye Valley Walk waymark post, go LEFT through the gate and across a small field and track by means of two further gates.

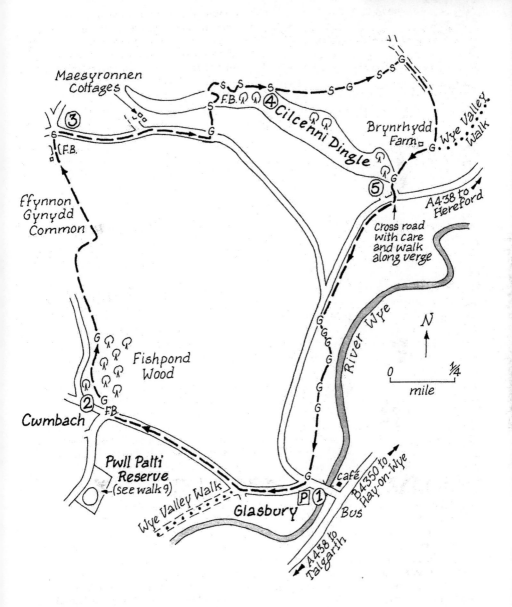

Head HALF RIGHT across the large field to a waymark post. Turn RIGHT and follow the riverside path through two more gates. Go half way along the next field and then go through a metal gate on the left. Continue along the edge of the field to a final gate and steps up to the A438. Cross with care to return to the car park.

WYE VALLEY WALK, FRON WOOD & GARTH DINGLE

DESCRIPTION This moderate route, of some 8 miles, follows a picturesque stretch of the Wye Valley Walk alongside the river, passing through level arable fields before heading for the small village of Llowes. The route follows the Wye Valley Walk up on to common land at Bryn yr Hydd, then turns off to follow a bridleway through the woods. Joining quiet lanes, the walk then leads to a footpath crossing fields to enter the Woodland Trust reserve at Fron Wood/Garth Dingle. Permissive paths lead through the wood, passing open stretches that allow viewpoints down onto the Wye valley. The permissive paths eventually lead out of the reserve back to Llowes, where the Wye Valley Walk can be followed back to Hay-on-Wye. Allow up to 6½ hours for the walk.
WEBSITE www.woodland-trust.org.uk
START Hay-on-Wye Town Clock, SO 229424.

2 Eventually, follow the Wye Valley Walk to the right across a narrow field. Go up the steps and through a kissing gate. The official route of the Wye Valley Walk now leads up further steps, but – if wishing to cut down on road walking – turn LEFT and follow the path to a lay-by. Continue west along the A438 to reach Llowes. Cross the main road with care and take the side road into

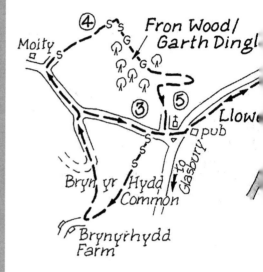

I From the pavement opposite the town clock, head LEFT and soon turn LEFT on the B4351 towards Clyro. Cross the Wye Bridge and continue along the B-road until reaching a Wye Valley Walk waymark post on the left. Go through the kissing gate and follow the Wye Valley Walk along the right hand side of the field to a gate into a small wood. Follow the waymarked path down to the right, alongside a high wall on the right. Bypass an old stile and head HALF RIGHT to reach a footbridge. Cross and turn LEFT on the track. Go past the entrance to a house and follow the Wye Valley Walk round to the right. Remain on the riverside path, which now leads across several large arable fields, affording views of the river and of the hills to the west. *The stiles along this section of the route have recently been removed, leaving gaps in the boundaries between fields.*

the village, passing the church on the right. Continue along the village street, looking out for a Wye Valley Walk signing to the left.

3 Go LEFT across a stile, continue AHEAD between fences and cross a second stile. Keeping the fence line to the right, continue AHEAD and then go up the bank to a stile below trees. Cross and follow the path up through the wood. On reaching two waymark posts (before the gate to Brynyrhydd Farm), leave the Wye Valley Walk and turn RIGHT onto the bridleway (not the footpath). Follow this through the wood to a lane. Turn RIGHT and follow the lane down to a junction with another lane. Turn LEFT and follow the lane for about ¼ mile, then go RIGHT on a no-through lane. Go past 'Moity' on the left. When the lane bends sharply to the left, cross the stile on the right.

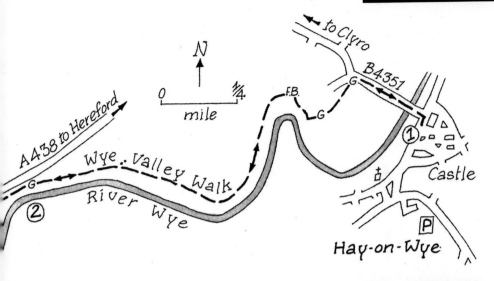

4 Head along the left hand side of the field to cross a stile into the wood. Follow the path AHEAD and then up the bank to a stile. Follow the treeline on the right. Go through a gate in a dip on the right and cross a small stream. Cross the next field, on a path between gorse bushes. Before reaching the end of the field, go through a gate on the right into Garth Dingle. Follow the track AHEAD for a short way, then go up steps on the left. Follow the path to, and across, another track near an entry gate into the wood. Continue to follow the path through the wood, eventually descending to the right. On reaching a broader track, turn LEFT. Follow the track down to a junction with a lane. Continue AHEAD to reach the road through Llowes village.

5 Turn LEFT and retrace the route to the main road. Cross with care and head LEFT along the verge until reaching the lay-by where the path can be followed back to the off-road section of the Wye Valley Walk. Go through the kissing gate, descend the steps and head back across the field to bear LEFT on the riverside path back to Hay-on-Wye. Shortly after passing the house on the right, go RIGHT over the footbridge, bear HALF RIGHT past the old stile and follow

the path up to the gate (*the first sight of Hay-on-Wye is worth a pause here*). Head along the left hand side of the field to a gate onto the road. Turn RIGHT and follow the road back down to Hay-on-Wye.

THE BEGWNS

DESCRIPTION A moderate walk of about 6 miles on National Trust owned upland with open access status, providing an excellent opportunity to walk hills frequented by ground-nesting birds and where buzzards can often be sighted. The conservation area also contains a lake – the setting of this will be familiar to readers of books such as 'The Moods of Kilvert Country' – and several ponds. There is the interesting feature of a circular drystone wall, enclosing a circular stone picnic 'bench'. The information board relating to the origin of this feature is currently absent, but it was built as a National Trust project to replace an earlier drystone wall. The ground cover consists mostly of turf, small patches of gorse and low-growing bracken. The walk directions that follow are a suggested route that takes in the main features of the Begwns and allows excellent views of Hay Bluff and the Black Mountains to the south and the hills to the north. Up to 4 hours should be allowed for the walk. The Begwyns are used for sheep grazing, so please keep dogs on leads. **WEBSITE** www.nationaltrust.org.uk **START** Roadside parking along the unfenced Glasbury to Painscastle road, in the area of SO 162440.

1 From the roadside parking, head west towards The Roundabout, plainly visible on the crest of the hill. There are a number of grassy tracks and sheep paths through the low-growing bracken that lead to The Roundabout. Access is via a stile near the National Trust trig point.

2 When ready, leave The Roundabout. Head past the trig point and continue roughly west down the hill. Head towards the first of the ponds visible ahead. *This section of the walk provides a range of views towards the farm land around Painscastle and the hills beyond.* Continue beyond the open surfaced pond to reach another, over-grown, pond.

3 From here, follow grassy tracks and sheep paths to the high ground along the western edge of the common. Turn south and follow the high ground until nearing a narrow strip of land between fences that leads onto a road.

4 Turn half LEFT here and follow a grassy track well marked with horse hoof prints that leads along the southern edge of the Begwns, crossing through an area of short turf. *This section of the route provides excellent views to the high land beyond Hay-on-Wye.* Follow the track across a ford and head half LEFT, passing below The Roundabout to return to the road.

5 Head, again on grassy tracks, for the area around the lake. Continue past this to follow tracks along the smaller eastern half of the common – *again, readers of Kilvert and books about the Victorian cleric will be familiar with some of the house names on Ordnance Survey maps for the area.* On nearing a road, double back to return to the Glasbury to Painscastle road.

The Roundabout

24

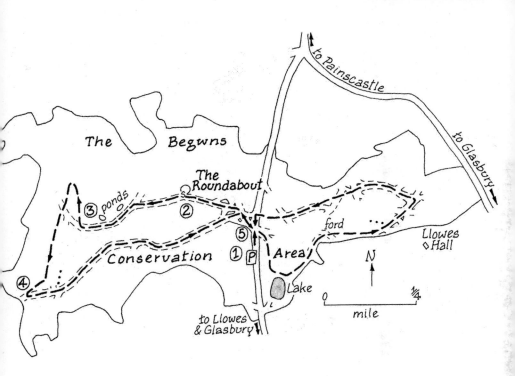

Meadow Pipit

Rather nondescript
streaked brown bird.
Evocative, tinkling
'pseet-pseet-pseet' call.
Nests in cup of grass
on the ground.

14-15 cm

Skylark

Similar in appearance
to Meadow Pipit, and
also nests in grassy
cup on the ground.
Familiar rolling 'chirrup'
call.

← short crest,
raised occasionally

18 cm

OFFA'S DYKE PATH & CWM BYDDOG

DESCRIPTION This moderate walk of 7 miles follows Offa's Dyke Path alongside the Wye and then across fields to enter the scenic Bettws Dingle. Heading up through the woods, the route then follows a quiet lane and minor road to the Radnorshire Wildlife Trust reserve at Cwm Byddog. The waymarked trails around this reserve currently appear to be in the process of being extended – at the time of writing there was a waymarked route of about 1¼ miles available. This reserve contains some of the oldest trees in Radnorshire, with pollarded oaks of up to 450 years old, one of which measures more than 20 feet about the girth. The reserve includes the site of a motte and bailey castle, that provides scrubland birds such as blackcap, garden warbler and yellowhammer. This is another excellent site for viewing wildflowers in the spring. From here the route continues by minor road to Clyro, where it crosses the main A438 to join an attractive waymarked footpath across fields back to the road near Hay-on-Wye. NB The bridleway starting near Cwm Byddog – although waymarked – is currently in poor condition, particularly at the end nearest to the main road. Use of this to return to Hay-on-Wye is not recommended. Allow up to 5¾ hours for the walk.
WEBSITE www.radnorshirewildlifetrust.org.uk
START The Town Clock, Hay-on-Wye, SO 229424

1 From the pavement opposite the town clock, head LEFT and soon turn LEFT towards Clyro. Cross the Wye Bridge. On reaching the Offa's Dyke Path sign, descend the steps on the right. After a few feet, take the left fork in the path and continue AHEAD through the wood. Cross a footbridge and follow the waymark sign HALF RIGHT. Cross a stile and follow a path AHEAD, leading gradually to the left. Follow a track beneath trees, passing a waymark post on the left. Continue along the riverside field, passing a small cairn on the left. Cross a stile and head along the next field, aiming only SLIGHTLY TO THE LEFT to reach a stile by a waymark post. Follow the path along the left hand side of the next large field. At the first waymark post, go LEFT through the gap. Immediately, follow the waymarked route to the right and continue AHEAD between hedges. Just before reaching a gate, cross the waymarked stile on the right.

2 Go down the steps and follow the waymarked path along the left hand side of the large field. Cross a waymarked stile to the right of a gate. Continue AHEAD across the field towards farm buildings. Cross a stile a few yards to the right of a gate. Cross the track to a second stile, just to the left of a gate. Pass a waymark post and follow the path HALF LEFT across the field. Cross a waymarked stile to the right of a gate. Follow the path HALF LEFT across the field to a stile below trees. Cross the stile, a footbridge and a second stile. Follow the path HALF RIGHT between trees and then HALF LEFT along the edge of the field. Go up the track, by a waymark post on the left. Follow the path HALF LEFT past two more waymark posts and up a bank to a stile onto the A438.

3 Turn RIGHT and walk along the broad verge (there is a clear path here) for about ¼ mile. Cross the main road with care and take the lane opposite, by Offa's Dyke Path waymark sign. Follow the lane uphill and take the right fork. Shortly thereafter, cross a stile to the left of the track and immediately follow the waymark sign to the left. Follow the path uphill past two more waymark posts and to the left of the trees. Cross a stile and follow the path through the edge of the wood. Ignore a footpath leading left, near a barn, and remain on Offa's Dyke Path. Follow the track over a bridge and uphill, past the next waymark post on the left. At a further two waymark posts, go LEFT and then SHARP LEFT.

4 Follow the track through conifers and then through an old gateway. Go up the steps to a lane. Turn LEFT and and follow the lane past Tump Farm, on the right. Go past the T-junction with a road coming from the right. Follow the road for about another mile. After passing Cwm Byddog House (on the left), look out for the turning on the left leading to Cwrt Evan Gwynne. Go a short way along the turning and then go through a gate on the left, into the nature reserve. Follow the path/s around the reserve, which are marked by white-topped posts. As noted above, path extension work appears to be taking place at the present time. On leaving the reserve, go RIGHT to the road and turn LEFT. Continue AHEAD for about half a mile, passing a lane coming from the right, to reach Clyro.

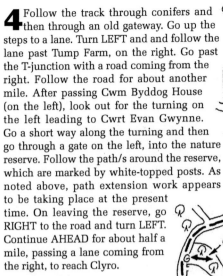

5 Just before reaching the main road, take the right fork into the village. *The Baskerville Arms Hotel is on the right, near the Post Office/shop.* When ready to leave Clyro, go along the path and then lane just to the left of the shop. Cross the main road with care towards the footpath sign opposite. Take the path to the right of the footpath sign, going through the gap in the hedge. Cross the driveway, aiming for the stile slightly to the left. Cross and head across the field, with the high ground and houses to the right. Continue beyond the high ground, to the left of old fencing and then continue AHEAD towards a line of trees on the right.

6 At the waymark post below the trees, head up the left hand side of the field to reach a stile (the direction indicated by the waymark arrow appears a little confusing at the present time). Cut across the next field to the far right hand corner. Do not take the track leading from the corner of the field, but bear RIGHT and go through the left hand of two gates. Go through and head across the field to a gate and then cross the next field to a stile. Head for the far right corner of another field. Cross the stile and follow the right hand side of the final field to a gate onto an access road. Go along this to reach the junction of road and main road. Turn LEFT on main road and follow pavement down to Hay-on-Wye.

27

BEACON HILL
COMMON

DESCRIPTION This moderate walk of some 4¾ miles (with an optional linear extension of up to 4 miles) crosses Beacon Hill Common, following Glyndŵr's Way and then turning off onto a bridleway leading up the trig point on Beacon Hill itself, the highest point of the Common. A Crown Estate, managed by Radnorshire Wildlife Trust, the Common consists of moorland composed mostly of bilberry, crowberry, heather, bracken (low growing on the hills) and acid grasses. It is home to a range of birds that include buzzard, curlew (in wetter areas), hen harrier (in winter), meadow pippit, peregrine, ring ousel, skylark, wheatear and whinchat. In addition to the wildlife interest, the Common provides a range of spectacular views. Access is restricted to walkers and horseriders on bridleways, with no vehicles other than those used by local graziers. This being common land, local people also enjoy rights to cut bracken, take stone and wood from the Common (known as 'rights of estover'). This is an early example of 'access land' in that a Crown Estate deed of 1932 gave the right to all to wander on foot across the Common. *The Common is used for grazing and walkers with dogs are requested to keep them under control.*
WEBSITE www.radnorshirewildlifetrust.org.uk
START Limited roadside parking alongside the upper part of the lane leading from the T-junction at SO 206738 to the entrance to Beacon Hill Common, SO 192748. Please take care not to block gateways when parking.

I From the B4356, turn north just to the west of Llangynllo village, following signs for the Railway Station (*NO PARKING AVAILABLE HERE*). Continue along the lane, passing a side-turning coming from the left, a phone box and Llangoch Farm. At the next junction, turn LEFT and head up the no-through lane, passing the entrance to Pen-y-bank, on the left. Having found a suitable parking place, continue to the end of the lane and go through the gate onto the Common.

2 Continue AHEAD towards the Beacon Hill Common information plaque, being joined by Glyndŵr's Way, which comes via the forestry area on the left. Follow the frequent Glyndŵr's Way signposts, passing Short Ditch, a single bank and ditch visible on both sides of the track. Follow the long distance route to the right of Pool Hill. After having followed Glyndŵr's Way for about two miles, look out for a track leading off to the right. This can be found just after having passed the valley on the left between Pool and Stankey Hills. Hoofprints show that the track is in regular use by horses. (If you wish to extend the walk, continue along Glyndŵr's Way. On the way back look out for a track leading uphill to the left just before descending to cross the valley between Sankey and Pool Hills, both to the right).

3 Follow the track uphill – it is faint in places but there are plenty of hoof prints to serve as visual reference points. The track now leads all the way up the trig point on Beacon Hill, *a good place to stop for a break and look at the extensive views.* When ready to leave, face away from the trig point and take the track to the left of and at approximately a 90 degree angle to the track followed on the way up. Follow this downhill, during which the track becomes clearer. Cross the brow of a rise and look ahead to see the forestry area close to the entry gate to the Common. Continue to descend towards the fields and turn RIGHT on reaching a cross-track.

4 Follow the main track AHEAD, crossing a small valley and skirting a damp area to reach a Glyndŵr's Way signpost near Pool Hill. Turn LEFT and follow the track back to the entry gate onto the Common.

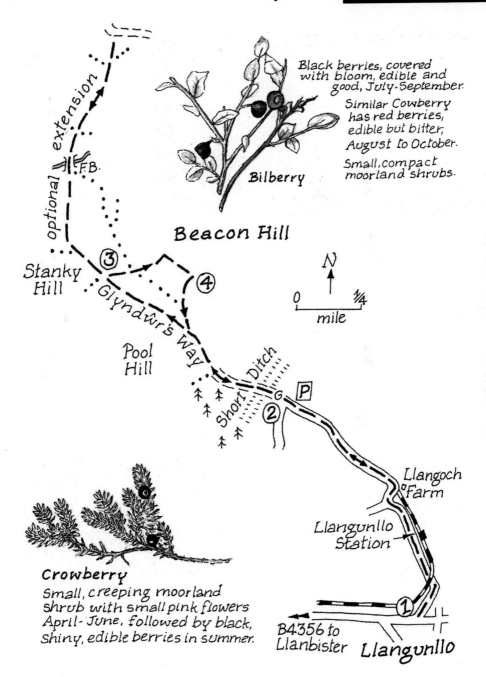

Black berries, covered
with bloom, edible and
good, July-September.

Similar Cowberry
has red berries,
edible but bitter,
August to October.

Small, compact
moorland shrubs.

Bilberry

Beacon Hill

optional extension

F.B.

Stanky Hill

③

④

Glyndŵr's Way

Pool Hill

Short Ditch

G ℗

②

N

0 ¼
mile

Llangoch Farm

Llangunllo Station

①

B4356 to
Llanbister **Llangunllo**

Crowberry
Small, creeping moorland
shrub with small pink flowers
April-June, followed by black,
shiny, edible berries in summer.

GRANNER WOOD & BURFABOG

DESCRIPTION This moderate walk of 4¼ or 4¾ miles leads east from the village of Evenjobb to visit a mixed wood owned by the Woodland Trust. Offa's Dyke Path runs through the wood, with a small section of the actual Dyke present at the start of this section of the walk. Offa's Dyke Path leads through the upper, coniferous, section of the wood (containing Douglas Fir, Japanese Larch and Noble Fir, with Scots Pine at the highest point) and links to another path running through the lower, decidous, area (containing sessile oaks). After this circular walk through the wood, the route then re-joins Offa's Dyke Path (and the course of the Dyke) for about ¾ mile. Offa's Dyke Path meanders along the boundaries of fields, following the Dyke which is frequently bordered by rows of trees, making an open-hedgerow type habitat. A short lane walk leads to the entrance to Radnorshire Wildife Trust's Burfabog Reserve, a mixture of streams, wetland, woods and rough grazing, with the site of a motte and bailey and an older tumulus. In addition to a wide range of wetland plants, the reserve has been recorded as used by 37 species of breeding birds, with the alder areas being visited in winter by finch species. On leaving the reserve, there is the choice of a lane walk back to Evenjobb or retracing the outward route along Offa's Dyke Path, with the latter adding ½ mile to the route. *Dogs are NOT allowed in Burfabog Reserve.*
WEBSITES www.radnorshirewildlifetrust.org. uk, www.woodland-trust.org.uk
START Roadside parking in Evenjobb village, SO 264624.

I From Evenjobb village, head east on the lane that leads towards Presteigne. Follow this uphill and past the mast on the right. Look out for steps on both sides of the lane, where Offa's Dyke Path crosses. Turn LEFT here and go up the steps. Follow the path to and up a second set of steps on the right. Follow the path to the left and

climb a third set of steps, again on the right. Turn LEFT on a broad track and after a few feet, bear RIGHT on a path next to an Offa's Dyke Path waymark post. Follow the path up to and along the top of the wood, passing through the mainly coniferous section.

2 On reaching a stile at the end of the wood, do not cross but turn LEFT and head downhill to the left of the fence. Turn LEFT on a grassy path leading through the lower, mainly deciduous, part of the wood. Continue along the this path when it becomes more hard surfaced to reach the point where Offa's Dyke Path crosses. Turn RIGHT down the steps and retrace the route back to the lane.

3 Turn LEFT and almost immediately go up the other steps on the right. Follow the clear route of Offa's Dyke Path as it heads along the Dyke, at the boundary of fields, connected by stiles. At one point, this route descends and re-ascends steps, possibly crossing an old gap in the Dyke. On reaching a lane, turn RIGHT and follow the lane to a T-junction. Bear LEFT and, when the lane bends to the left, look for a kissing gate on the right. Go through and head LEFT past the Radnorshire Wildlife Trust information board, to another gate.

4 Go through the gate and follow the boardwalk to the further gate. Follow the path across the field, to the right of the enclosed young trees to reach the motte and bailey remains. Follow the path to the right of the mound and cross another gated board-walk. Follow the path across the clearing and through trees to reach a third gated board-walk. Cross and continue AHEAD to reach a boardwalk without gates. Start across the next clearing and turn RIGHT to cross a further ungated boardwalk. Head to the right of the trees to reach a fourth gated boardwalk. Cross the field and go RIGHT on a final gated boardwalk. Head along the left hand side of the field to reach the entrance to the reserve. To take the short route back, turn LEFT and follow the main lane to a T-junction on the edge of Evenjobb, turning left into the village.

Noble Fir
Native of NW
Pacific coast of
America.
Formal appearance
with straight stem
and bluish foliage.

Scots Pine
Native of Scottish
Highlands.
Distinctive round,
spreading, head.
Bark orange to pink
towards top of trunk.

Japanese Larch
Native of Japan.
Deciduous tree.
Slender blue-green
leaves open in
early spring and
turn yellow in
autumn.

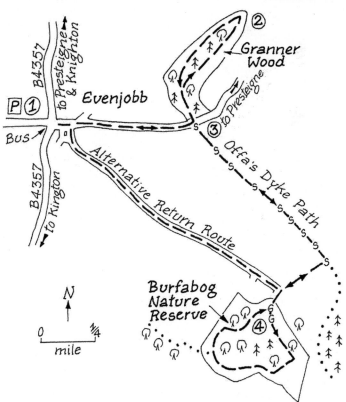

MAELIENYDD & COXHEAD BANK COMMON

DESCRIPTION This is a moderate walk of about 7½ miles, for which up to 5 hours should be allowed. It is a good example of a working landscape in which conservation is practised, being common land (now open access land) used for grazing in which controlled burning of selected areas of gorse is used to produce a range of vegetation habitats. For the most part (other than on Coxhead Bank) the Common is free of bracken and mainly consists of heather, gorse and rough grasses, with trees being found in hidden valleys and borders around the Common. Ground nesting birds make use of the area and red kites, buzzards and corvids can be seen overhead. There are also three (sometimes four) pools – Caergynan, Black (mostly concealed by vegetation) and two, unnamed, pools, one in the middle of the Common and one not far from the Castle Coch lane. The River Aran crosses the eastern part of the Common. The route below visits the features described above, while making use of some of the easier to follow tracks and paths across the Common.

START Roadside parking near the eastern end of the Common, circa SO 164714.

1 Follow the B4356 between Llanbister and Llangynllo. Immediately south of where the B-road passes under the railway line, take the minor road heading west (roughly parallel to the railway line). Go over the railway bridge just to the west of the request halt at Llanbister Road (if arriving by train, go up the steps from the station and immediately turn RIGHT). THERE IS NO PARKING AVAILABLE AT THE STATION. Follow the lane for about ¾ mile to reach a cattlegrid onto the Common. Cross and turn RIGHT on an unfenced lane, parking in this area if arriving by car. Take a parallel course to the lane, keeping to its left until passing a track leading off to the right. Cross the lane and now follow the right hand side of the

Common to reach a tree-lined stream gulley. Turn LEFT and walk along the high ground to the left of the gulley to rejoin the lane.

2 Turn RIGHT and follow the lane across the River Aran bridge. Almost immediately, bear HALF LEFT across open ground (approximately mid-way between the lane and a track leading off to the left). Go uphill past the poles and then head for a three-way signpost at the junction of lanes (this cuts off a bend in the lane). At the junction, follow the right hand lane, signposted for Castle Coch. Look out for the site of a small pool on the left, while following the unfenced lane. After passing Blaen--cwm (on the right), look out for a grassy path leading half left. Follow this and soon turn SHARP LEFT on a grassy vehicle track. On reaching a clear area, with a field gate off to the right, bear SHARP LEFT on another grassy track.

3 At the end of the track, continue AHEAD on sheep paths, crossing the head of two gulleys to the right - the distinctive shape of Gaer, with its hilltop fort, makes a good visual reference point ahead. Pass a single rowan tree and turn LEFT on a path. On reaching a junction of paths, turn RIGHT. At the next junction of paths, now in sight of the lane, turn LEFT. Follow sheep paths across the

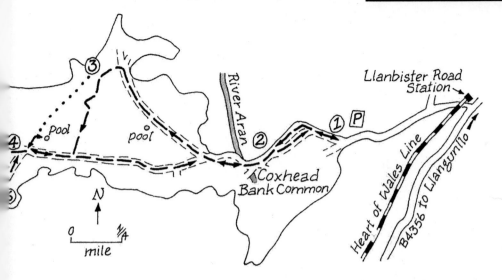

hill (there is a smalll pile of stones to mark the 361 metre summit) and down to the lane. Follow the lane to the right – if you wish to visit the small pool seen from the hill, take a path leading to the right before reaching the junction ahead. Follow this for a while and then bear right, retracing the outward route when ready. Continue west for a short way to reach the junction.

4 Turn LEFT and immediately turn RIGHT on a grassy track. At a junction of tracks, go RIGHT. Cross the brow of hills and then descend, with Caergynan Pool off to the left. Divert left to visit the pool, returning to the track when ready. Continue downhill, taking the right fork at a junction of tracks. The route is faint here for a while – Gaer should be visible well to the left. Keep to the most right hand of several vehicle tracks across the Common and then follow the right hand side of a sizeable stream gully to reach a lane. Turn LEFT and, once beyond the gulley, turn LEFT again and follow the high ground to the left of the stream. On reaching a small valley, on the right, turn RIGHT and use sheep paths to reach a grassy vehicle track. Turn LEFT on this and go along the hill. At the junction with a well-used vehicle track, turn LEFT again and follow the track to a lane.

5 Turn RIGHT on the lane and go down a small hill. Turn LEFT on a track that leads towards Black Pool (this can be glimpsed near trees to the left). After visiting the pool area – care needed as much of the pool, including the edge, is concealed – retrace the outward route to the lane and turn RIGHT. Follow the lane as far as the cattlegrid where it leaves the Common. Rather than crossing the cattlegrid, turn LEFT here and follow a track along the boundary of the Common (this once again gives a view of Caergynan Pool and Bank to the left). Skirt the enclosed land on the right by going HALF LEFT up Caergynan Bank and then following the main track round to the right. Descend to join a lane and turn LEFT.

6 Follow the lane to a T-junction and turn RIGHT. Follow the lane until nearing the junction with the lane to Castle Coch. Again, cut across the open ground on the right, leading down to the River Aran Bridge. Turn RIGHT and follow the lane over the bridge and back to the T-junction near the cattlegrid leading off the Common. Head LEFT over the grid and retrace the outward route past, or to, Llanbister Road station (request stop).

WALK 18
MYNYDD FFOESIDOES

DESCRIPTION This moderate 5½ mile route follows a well used bridleway and then a path along the side of a wild valley and across open moorland, with some spectacular views, to Radnorshire Wildlife Trust's Mynydd Ffoesidoes Reserve. There is a good opportunity to compare the ungrazed upland heath in the reserve to the surrounding area to which sheep do have access. The reserve contains cowberry, crowberry, heather and lesser amounts of bilberry, together with rushes and other herbaceous plants. A wet area, towards the centre of the reserve, contains small pools where mosses, lichens and other wetland plants can be seen. Bird life includes Meadow Pipit, Skylark and Tree Pipit, while buzzards and red kites may be seen overhead. The reserve is a good location for beetles – over 40 species have been recorded. Allow up to 4½ hours for the walk.

There is no waymarked route around the Reserve. The distance given above refers to the length of route to and from the entrance.

The Reserve is used by ground nesting birds. Please keep dogs on SHORT leads. Larger groups of visitors are requested to contact the Trust (01597 823298) prior to visiting the Reserve.

WEBSITE www.radnorshirewildlifetrust.org.uk
START Broadwell Forest Parking Area, one mile north of New Radnor, SO 205619.

From the B4372 at New Radnor, follow Mutton Dingle (no through lane) for about one mile north, to the parking area near the entrance to Broadwell Forest.

Follow the access track back down to the lane and turn RIGHT onto the bridleway running to the west of Broadwell Forest. Cross a stile and follow the grassy track uphill to the left of the forest.

2 On reaching the end of the forest, continue AHEAD on the clear track. Go through a gate and continue AHEAD on the track, climbing to a second gate, within site of the forestry plantation ahead. Once through the second gate, bear HALF LEFT and then HALF LEFT again. Follow the track up past the poles and continue along the track, now running to the right of a fence.

3 Continue along the track, making for the Black Mixen Mast. Leave the track shortly before reaching the mast and head LEFT to the nearby trig point. Go past the trig point and follow a clear path, the route of which is marked by three wooden posts, for the last half mile or so, to the fence on the right that marks the boundary of the nature reserve. Follow the fence to a stile into the forestry plantation. Cross this and double back to the right. Follow the other side of the fence to reach a stile into the nature reserve.

4 When ready, leave the reserve and follow the fence back towards the forestry plantation. Cross the stile on the left and follow the path back to the Mast and trig point. Rejoin the track just beyond the trig point and follow this to the right. Follow the track along the left hand side of the fence and down past the poles. Bear RIGHT to return to the gate passed through earlier. Retrace the route down through a further gate and over a stile to return to the lane near Broadwell Forest.

Ground Beetle

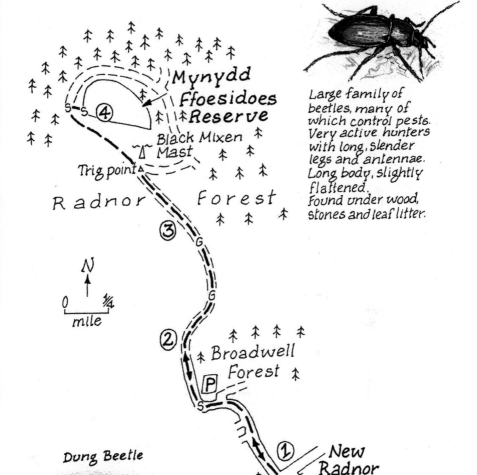

Large family of
beetles, many of
which control pests.
Very active hunters
with long, slender
legs and antennae.
Long body, slightly
flattened.
Found under wood,
stones and leaf litter.

Mynydd
Ffoesidoes
Reserve

Black Mixen
Mast

Trig point

R a d n o r   F o r e s t

④

③

②

N

0 ——— ¼
mile

Broadwell
Forest

P

①   New
Radnor

pub   Bus-
(Llandrindod
-Hereford)

to
Rhayader   A44   to
Kington

Dung Beetle

Small, stout insects,
all broadly oblong
in shape with strong,
spiny, legs which are
used for digging tunnels
beneath dung. pieces
of which are carried
down to feed their
larvae.

HERGEST RIDGE & LLANHAYLOW WOOD

DESCRIPTION This moderate walk is comprised of some 9 miles, plus a variety of paths around one of the Woodland Trust's Radnorshire Reserves. Starting from a lane just outside the Herefordshire town of Kington, the walk follows Offa's Dyke Path (no sign of the Dyke itself here, just some incredible views and a variety of upland birds) before crossing into Wales and descending to Gladestry. From here, a quiet lane walk leads to Llanhaylow Wood, where there are a variety of paths that can be used to make circular routes of different lengths through this mixed but now mainly deciduous woodland. Llanhaylow is an ancient woodland site, with sessile oak, beech, birch, douglas fir, hawthorn, hazel, poplar and rowan. Goldcrest, great spotted woodpecker and tawny owl have been sighted here and the wood is especially worth a visit in spring for its array of woodland flowers including primroses, bluebells and early purple orchids. Specific features of interest include ponds, streams and a fallen willow bypassed by steps. The paths are cleared twice a year – to check current status, use website address provided below. Allow some 6 hours for the walk.
WEBSITE www.woodland-trust.org.uk
START Ridgebourne Road, edge of Kington, SO 282568

From roadside parking in Ridgebourne Road, follow the road up to a gate onto Hergest Ridge. Go through and follow the left hand track uphill to reach the first of the Offa's Dyke Path waymark signs (generally blue arrow/white acorn) that show the course of the long distance trail across the Ridge. Pass the Memorial Bench to John and Mary Grist. *In addition to the upland bird life, look out for Black Mixen Mast (above New Radnor) off to the right and, looking left, Hay Bluff beyond Hay-on-Wye.*

2 Pass a four-way waymark post. Soon after this, the distinctive shape of Hanter Hill appears on the right. Pass a second four-way post. When the track divides, by a valley to the right, take the left fork which soon brings you to a waymark post. Continue towards a hill top waymark post. The stone marker posts from this point on are an indication that the route has returned to Wales. Pass a hill top pond on the right and begin to descend. Just before reaching the final hill, at the Offa's Dyke Path waymark signs, bear HALF LEFT and follow the track down hill to a gate.

3 Go through onto unfenced lane and follow this down through a second gate. Continue down hill on the lane and turn RIGHT at the first junction. Turn LEFT at the second junction and go past the pub and Post Office/shop. At the village green, go RIGHT. Follow the lane past the church and continue ahead for about ¾ mile. When lane bends to left, turn RIGHT to see the welcome and information boards provided by the Woodland Trust. There are two ways to enter the woodland, but to follow the route suggested, follow directions in stage 4 below. (This does not take in the path at the very eastern end of the reserve, as will be seen from the map on the information board).

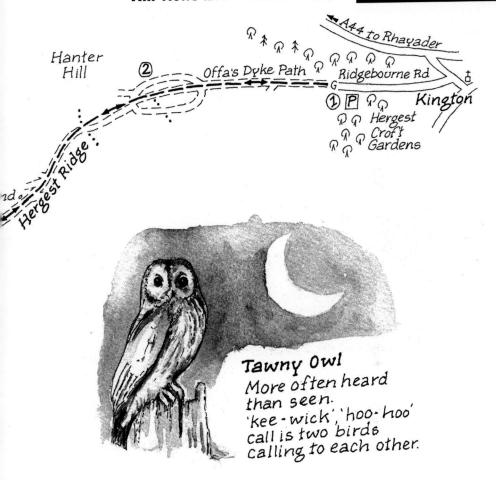

Hanter
Hill

② - - - - Offa's Dyke Path

A44 to Rhayader

Ridgebourne Rd

① P Kington

Hergest
Croft
Gardens

Hergest Ridge

Tawny Owl
More often heard
than seen.
'kee-wick', 'hoo-hoo'
call is two birds
calling to each other.

4 Return to lane and follow this to the right for a few feet. Turn RIGHT on the track and follow this for some way until coming to an entry gap, by wooden fencing on the right. Go into the wood and follow the path (unwaymarked but easy enough to see). At the steep descent, go down the steps and cross a footbridge. Ignore the second set of steps on the right and continue AHEAD, using short flights of steps to skirt a tree branch across the path. Continue AHEAD to reach a clearing and then turn RIGHT on a path back into the woods. At the next junction of paths, turn LEFT over footbridge.

Continue AHEAD, taking care at the start of a steep section – the steps currently start part way down. At the bottom of the steps, turn LEFT. Go over the first footbridge and then go HALF LEFT up the steps. Follow the path back out of the wood and turn LEFT on the track back to the lane. Follow the lane back to Gladestry, going LEFT at the Green and RIGHT after the pub. Bear HALF LEFT on the lane, going through two gates on to the track. At the two Offa's Dyke Path waymark posts, bear RIGHT and follow the track back along the ridge to the gate onto Ridgebourne Road.

WALK 20

WITHYBEDS, WENTES MEADOW, THE WARREN & SILIA WOOD

DESCRIPTION This easy 3½ mile walk (with some steps in the Silia Wood section) is located in the attractive small border town of Presteigne, in which there are a variety of other places to visit, such as the interactive Judge's Lodging Museum/TIC. The route visits a Radnorshire Wildlife Trust reserve that combines riverside and wet woodland, with vegetation comprised of canopy, shrub and field layers (Withybeds) and meadow, pond and mill leat (Wentes Meadow) before going on to the Warren (the site of a Marcher motte and bailey castle) where there is a circular path through woods. One of the two information boards at the Warren includes a distinctive month by month display of flowers, fruits and berries that can be seen at particular times. From there the walk continues by lane to the Woodland Trust property at Silia Wood, a mixed wood through which there are a variety of paths. Some sections of this are covered by means of steps. As well as oak and ash, Silia includes non-native species such as box, butcher's broom and flowering currants. A lane route is then followed back to the town centre. Allow up to 2¼ hours for the walk. *Walkers with dogs are requested to keep them on a lead in Silia wood, where paths have been designed to avoid going near the main entrances to the badger setts.*
WEBSITES www.radnorshirewildlifetrust.org. uk, www.woodland-trust.org.uk
START The junction of Broad Street and High Street, Presteigne, SO 315644

I Head down Broad Street (located between the Llanandras Post Office and the Assembly Rooms) passing the Judge's Lodging to reach the church on the left. Enter the church grounds and follow the path to the left of the church to reach a lane. Turn LEFT on the lane, passing a 'Nature Trail' signpost (a tall green post).

2 Go RIGHT at the first junction and continue AHEAD at the second. Follow the lane ahead and then take a waymarked path slightly to the left, just before a house down a track to the right. Just before reaching a gate, go RIGHT down steps and over a footbridge, passing a Radnorshire Wildlife Trust information board on the left. Follow the circular walk (mostly on boardwalk) around the Withybeds section of the reserve. *This part of the reserve runs alongside the River Lugg, itself a Site of Special Scientific Interest and home to otters. The woodland, which floods in winter, was formerly the source of willow for the local basket-makers and consists of canopy, shrub and field layers, including places where saplings grow on the remains of fallen trees.*

3 Access Wentes Meadow by a gate at the western end of Withybeds. *Hay is cut here every July and there is occasional grazing to improve the pasture.* There is a path around the pond and leat area in the centre of the meadow, where there are additional information boards. *These features were created in 1992, when the old mill leat was excavated and is now home to considerable invertebrate populations, such as over 70 species of beetles.* When ready, return most of the way along the outward path. Just before reaching the lane and the house on the left, turn RIGHT and go up steps to a path between field fences.

Silia Wood

4 Turn LEFT on the road and look out for a footpath sign on the right. Go up the drive past the house and continue up steps to the main road. Cross with care and head into Warren Road. Follow this round to the right, ignoring the first path on the right. Turn through a gate on the right and follow the path up to the right, passing the first of the two information boards. Follow the path

38

Withybeds
& Wentes Moor
Nature Reserve

N

0 _____ ¼
mile

River Lugg

The Warren

High Street

P.O.

Broad St.

Judges Lodging
Museum
& T.I.C.

PRESTEIGNE

Warrengate Rd. ⑤

school

Slough Road

around the Warren, passing the second information board with its monthly 'what to look for' calendar and return to Warren Road.

5 Turn LEFT and soon turn RIGHT into Castle Road. Follow this to the junction with Slough Road and turn RIGHT. Follow Slough Road for about half a mile, then go through a gate on the right (with a Woodland Trust sign) and follow a path on the right between hedges to reach Silia Wood. There are a variety of paths within the wood – one option is to take the path on the left and fol-

low a course roughly parallel to the boundary of the wood. This passes viewpoints (sometimes a short way off the main path) with benches and makes use of steps on steeper parts of the wood. *Nesting boxes have been provided for both bats and birds the latter including Great Spotted Woodpeckers, Long Tailed Tits, Nuthatches, Tawny Owls and Treecreepers. The wood is also a good area to see spring flowers.* When ready return along Slough Road to the junction with the main road. Bear to the RIGHT and go through the underpass (attractive murals for a change) and follow the road AHEAD back to the junction of Broad and High Streets.

PRONUNCIATION

These basic points should help non-Welsh speakers

Welsh	English equivalent
c	always hard, as in cat
ch	as on the Scottish word loch
dd	as th in then
f	as in of
ff	as in off
g	always hard as in got
ll	no real equivalent. It is like 'th' in then, but with an 'L' sound added to it, giving 'thlan' for the pronunciation of the Welsh 'Llan'.

In Welsh the accent usually falls on the last-but-one syllable of a word.

KEY TO THE MAPS

- → Walk route and direction
- ═══ Metalled road
- ≡≡≡ Unsurfaced road
- •••• Footpath/route adjoining walk route
- 〰 River/stream
- ⚘ ♔ Trees
- G Gate
- S Stile
- F.B. Footbridge
- ▬ Railway
- P Parking
- T Telephone

THE COUNTRYSIDE CODE

- Be safe – plan ahead and follow any signs
- Leave gates and property as you find them
- Protect plants and animals, and take your litter home
- Keep dogs under close control
- Consider other people

The Countryside & Rights of Way Act 2000, implemented throughout Wales in May 2005, introduced new legal rights of access for walkers to designated open country, predominantly mountain, moor, heath or down, plus all registered common land. This access can be subject to restrictions and closure for land management or safety reasons for up to 28 days a year.

Published by **Kittiwake**
3 Glantwymyn Village Workshops, Glantwymyn, Machynlleth, Montgomeryshire SY20 8LY

© Text & map research: Jane Griffiths 2009
© Maps & illustrations: Kittiwake 2009
Maps & illustrations: Morag Perrott
Cover photos: *Main* – The Hergest Ridge (Walk 19): inset – Gilfach Farm Reserve (Walk 4). David Perrott

Care has been taken to be accurate. However neither the author nor the publisher can accept responsibility for any errors which may appear, or their consequences. If you are in any doubt about access, check before you proceed.

Printed by MWL, Pontypool.

ISBN: **978 1 902302 73 7**